# HEALTHY COOKING FOR BEGINNERS

*35 easy step-by-step recipes*

# Table of Contents

# Introduction

You don't have to spend the afternoon creating complicated and intricate dishes to enjoy a healthy diet.

USING THIS BOOK FOR BETTER HEALTH

If you are trying to eat healthier or lose weight, consider each recipe's nutrition information, including calories, total fat, saturated fat, protein, carbohydrates, fiber, and sodium. You can also keep an eye on each recipe's listed serving sizes, such as 1 piece, ¼ cup, or 2 tablespoons. This helps guide you in portion control, so you can stick to the amount that's considered a reasonable serving.

Each recipe is also labeled if it meets the criteria for any of the following:

*Gluten-Free:* These recipes do not contain wheat, rye, or barley. Some ingredients, like oats, do not contain gluten but may be processed in a facility that also processes wheat. Always read the label to check if your food is gluten-free. If it is processed in a facility containing wheat, the label must disclose this information.

*Dairy-Free:* These recipes do not contain milk or dairy foods, including cheese, ice cream, cottage cheese, and yogurt.

*Paleo-Friendly:* These recipes do not contain grains, white flour, dairy, legumes, refined sugar, yeast, vinegar, or pickled foods.

*Vegan:* These recipes do not contain any food derived from an animal, including meat, poultry, seafood, dairy, eggs, and honey.

*Vegetarian:* These recipes do not contain meat, poultry, or seafood. They may contain eggs and dairy.

NEW RECIPES EVERY WEEK

The recipes in this book are fun, healthy, and easy to prepare. Each week, the recipes change to incorporate new ingredients or blend different flavors.

## RELAX AND ENJOY

Recipes from women with busy schedules will help ensure that a new recipe finds its way into your weeknight meal rotation. You won't have to spend hours in the kitchen creating complicated meals; you'll just pull together a healthy dish that is always fast and easy to prepare.

# Chapter 1:
# Healthy Cooking Techniques

It's not only the food in the recipe but also how you cook it that makes a difference. Here are some techniques that work well for cooking healthy meals.

*Baking:* Baking is usually synonymous with desserts and breakfast items, but you can also bake seafood, lean meat, poultry, fruits, and vegetables. Baking doesn't usually require the addition of fat, but it's important to keep an eye on the time to avoid overbaking, which can dry out food. To bake a food, place it in a pan or ovenproof dish, covered or uncovered, for the specified duration of time.

*Grilling:* This is an excellent way to cook meat, poultry, seafood, vegetables, and fruits. Grilling allows fat to drip off, and it also browns the food, adding flavor.

*Poaching:* This cooking technique involves submerging food into water or a flavored liquid (like broth) to cook. Fish, eggs, chicken, and some fruits and vegetables can be poached.

*Roasting:* This technique is used for cooking vegetables as well as larger cuts of meat, poultry, and fish. Roasting brings out flavors in vegetables that can't be duplicated by other methods. When roasting meats, it's recommended to place the meat or poultry on a rack to allow the fat to drip off.

*Steaming:* This easy method for cooking vegetables, fruits, fish, shellfish, and chicken breasts doesn't require fat. To steam, cover the bottom of a medium pot with water and fit with a steamer basket filled with food. Bring the water to a boil, then reduce to a simmer. Cover the pot and cook until the food is cooked through.

*Sautéing:* This cooking method uses a small amount of fat to cook food quickly over high heat. When sautéing, use a shallow pan to let the moisture escape and leave room between the food items in the pan.

*Stir-frying:* Typically used to prepare Asian-style dishes, stir-frying involves cooking small pieces of food over high heat with a small amount of oil. This quick, high-heat method also preserves the crispness, bright color, and nutrients in the food.

# Chapter 2:
# Smoothies and Breakfasts

### Blueberry-Spinach Smoothie

Prep & Cooking time: 35 minutes

Servings: 1

### Ingredients:

- 1 cup of frozen blueberries
- 2 cups spinach, washed and patted dry
- ½ cup nonfat plain Greek yogurt
- ½ cup 100% apple juice
- 1 teaspoon of honey

### Directions:

1. In a blender, add the blueberries, spinach, yogurt, apple juice, and honey, and blend until smooth. Pour into a tall glass and serve.

2. TOBY'S TIP: When purchasing frozen fruit, make sure it has no added sugar by reading through the ingredient list or looking for "No added sugar" on the label.

*Serving size:* 14 fluid ounces

*Per serving:* Calories: 232; Total fat: 1 g; Saturated fat: 0 g; Protein: 14 g; Carbohydrates: 45 g; Fiber: 6 g; Sodium: 99 mg

# Grape-Melon Smoothie

Prep & Cooking time: 30 minutes

Servings: 1

## Ingredients:

- 1 cup of diced honeydew
- 1 cup of diced cantaloupe
- 1 cup of green seedless grapes
- ¼ cup 100% orange juice
- Juice of 1 lime
- 1 teaspoon of honey

## Directions:

1. In a blender, add the honeydew, cantaloupe, grapes, orange juice, lime juice, and honey, and blend until smooth. Pour into a tall glass and serve.

*Serving size:* 16 fluid ounces

*Per serving:* Calories: 242; Total fat: 1 g; Saturated fat: 0 g; Protein: 3 g; Carbohydrates: 61 g; Fiber: 4 g; Sodium: 45 mg.

# Tropical Protein Smoothie

Prep & Cooking time: 25 minutes

Servings: 1

**Ingredients**:

- ¾ cup diced frozen pineapple
- ¾ cup fresh baby kale rinsed and patted dry
- ¾ cup diced fresh or frozen mango
- ½ cup low-fat cottage cheese
- ½ cup skim milk or light coconut milk
- 1 teaspoon of honey

**Directions**:

1. In a blender, add the pineapple, kale, mango, cottage cheese, milk, and honey, and blend until smooth. Pour into a tall glass and serve.

*Serving size:* 16 fluid ounces

*Per serving:* Calories: 349; Total fat: 4 g; Saturated fat: 1 g; Protein: 21 g; Carbohydrates: 60 g; Fiber: 7 g; Sodium: 445 mg

# Cherry-Banana Smoothie

Prep& Cooking time: 25 minutes

Servings: 1

## Ingredients:

- 1 medium banana
- ½ cup frozen pitted sweet cherries
- ½ cup nonfat plain Greek yogurt
- ½ cup nonfat milk or almond milk
- ½ teaspoon vanilla extract or ground nutmeg

## Directions:

1. In a blender, add the banana, cherries, yogurt, milk, and vanilla or ground nutmeg, and blend until smooth. Pour into a tall glass and serve.

*Serving size:* 14 fluid ounces

*Per serving:* Calories: 255; Total fat: 0 g; Saturated fat: 0 g; Protein: 17 g; Carbohydrates: 49 g; Fiber: 5 g; Sodium: 98 mg

# Mexican-Style Potato Hash and Eggs

Prep & Cooking time: 45 minutes

Servings: 6

## Ingredients:

- 3 large russet potatoes
- 2 tablespoons of olive oil
- ½ teaspoon salt
- ¼ teaspoon freshly ground black pepper
- 6 large eggs
- 6 tablespoons shredded pepper Jack cheese
- 1 avocado, pitted, peeled, and cubed
- 6 tablespoons chopped fresh cilantro

## Directions:

2. Peel and grate the potatoes, and drain the excess liquid.

3. Preheat the broiler.

4. In a large, oven-safe skillet over medium-high heat, heat the olive oil. When the oil is shimmering, add the grated potatoes. Cook the potatoes, stirring occasionally until slightly browned and cooked through, about 10 minutes. Add the salt and pepper, and toss to combine.

5. Using a wooden spoon, create 6 evenly spaced wells in a circular pattern in the potato hash. Crack 1 egg into a wineglass. Gently pour the egg into a well. Repeat with the remaining eggs. Reduce heat to medium-low,

cover the skillet, and cook until the eggs are cooked through about 12 minutes.

6.  Uncover the skillet, and sprinkle each egg with 1 tablespoon of cheese. Place the uncovered skillet in the broiler for 2 minutes, until the cheese has melted and is slightly browned. Remove from the broiler.

7.  On each of the 6 plates, spoon 1 egg with one-sixth of the hash on a plate. Top each with 1 tablespoon of avocado and 1 tablespoon of chopped cilantro and serve.

*Serving size:* 1 egg plus ⅙ of the hash

*Per serving:* Calories: 320; Total fat: 17 g; Saturated fat: 4 g; Protein: 12 g; Carbohydrates: 33 g; Fiber: 7 g; Sodium: 345 mg

## Egg in a Hole

Prep & Cooking time: 20 minutes

Servings: 4

### Ingredients:

- 4 slices 100% whole-wheat bread
- 2 teaspoons of unsalted butter, at room temperature
- Cooking spray
- 4 large eggs
- 1 (¾-ounce) slice provolone cheese
- 1 tomato, cut crosswise into 4 slices
- ¼ teaspoon salt
- ⅛ teaspoon freshly ground black pepper

## Directions:

1. Using a cookie cutter or the top of a round glass, cut a hole in the center of each slice of bread. Reserve the centers of the bread for another use.

2. Spread ½ teaspoon of butter on each of the slices of bread.

3. Coat a nonstick skillet with cooking spray and heat over medium-high heat. When the cooking spray is shimmering, place the bread (buttered-side up) in the skillet. Crack 1 egg into a wineglass. Gently pour the egg into the center hole of 1 slice of bread. Repeat with the 3 remaining eggs and bread. Cook until the eggs are set, about 3 minutes, and carefully flip over each piece.

4. Gently place 1 slice of cheese and 1 slice of tomato onto the egg, and continue cooking an additional 3 minutes, until the eggs are cooked through and the cheese has slightly melted. Sprinkle the top of each tomato slice with salt and pepper. Serve immediately.

*Serving size:* 1 egg in a hole

*Per serving:* Calories: 228; Total fat: 14 g; Saturated fat: 7 g; Protein: 14 g; Carbohydrates: 13 g; Fiber: 2 g; Sodium: 333 mg

# Broccoli-Cheddar Egg Muffins

Prep & Cooking time: 45 minutes

Servings: 12

## Ingredients:

- Equipment: Steamer basket
- Cooking spray
- 2 cups broccoli florets
- 12 large eggs
- ½ cup skim milk or almond milk
- 3 scallions, chopped
- ½ teaspoon salt
- ¼ teaspoon freshly ground black pepper
- ¾ cup shredded low-fat Cheddar cheese

## Directions:

1. Preheat the oven to 350°F. Spray 12 muffin liners with cooking spray or place a liner in each cup of a 12-muffin tin.

2. Fill a medium pot with about an inch of water. Fit a steamer basket into the pot, and add the broccoli florets. Cover and heat over medium-high heat for about 5 minutes, until the broccoli, is crisp. Transfer the broccoli to a cutting board and allow to cool for 5 minutes, then chop the florets.

3. In a large bowl, whisk together the eggs, milk, scallions, salt, and pepper. Add the chopped broccoli, and toss to combine.

4. Spoon ⅓ cup of egg mixture into each of the prepared muffin liners, and top each with 1 tablespoon of shredded cheese.

5. Bake until the tops are golden brown, about 25 minutes. Let the muffins cool for 10 minutes before removing them from the tin. Serve while still warm.

6. To freeze, place the egg muffins in a single row in a freezer-safe container in the freezer for up to 2 months. To defrost, refrigerate overnight. Reheat in a 350°F oven for 5 to 10 minutes. Alternatively, reheat egg muffins in the microwave on high for 45 to 60 seconds and allow them to cool for 2 minutes before eating.

*Serving size:* 1 muffin

*Per serving:* Calories: 100; Total fat: 6 g; Saturated fat: 2 g; Protein: 9 g; Carbohydrates: 2 g; Fiber: 0 g; Sodium: 229 mg

## Parmesan Omelet

Prep & Cooking Time: 15 minutes

Servings: 2

**<u>Ingredients</u>:**

- 1 tablespoon of cream cheese
- 2 eggs, beaten
- ¼ teaspoon paprika
- ½ teaspoon dried oregano
- ¼ teaspoon dried dill
- 1 oz. Parmesan, grated
- 1 teaspoon of coconut oil

**Directions**:

1. Mix up together cream cheese with eggs, dried oregano, and dill.

2.Put coconut oil in the frypan and heat it until it coats all the skillet.

3. Then pour the egg mixture into the skillet and flatten it.

4. Add grated Parmesan and close the lid.

5. Cook the omelet for 10 minutes over low heat.

6. Then transfer the cooked omelet to the serving plate and sprinkle it with the paprika.

Nutrition: Calories: 148; Fat: 11.5 g; Fiber: 0.3 g; Carbs: 1.4 g; Protein: 10.6 g

## Omelet with New York Strip Steak

Prep & Cooking time: 30 minutes

Servings: 6

**Ingredients**:

- 2 tablespoons butter, at room temperature
- 1 ½ pound of New York strip cut into cubes Flaky
- Sea salt and pepper, to season
- 1/2 teaspoon smoked paprika
- 1/2 cup scallions, chopped
- 2 garlic cloves, pressed
- 2 Spanish peppers, deveined and chopped
- 6 eggs

## Directions:

1. In a frying pan, melt the butter over moderately high heat. Cook the beef until browned on all sides or for 10 to 12 minutes.

2. Season with salt, pepper, and paprika; reserve. In the same pan, cook the scallions, garlic, and pepper until just tender and aromatic. Add in the eggs and gently stir to combine. Continue to cook, covered, for 10 minutes more or until the eggs are set. Bon appétit!

Nutritional value per serving: 429 Calories; 27.8 g Fat; 3.2 g Carbs; 39.1 g Protein; 0.8 g Fiber

# Chapter 3:
# Main meal

**Curry Apple Couscous with Leeks and Pecans**

Prep & Cooking Time: 25 minutes

Servings: 4

**<u>Ingredients</u>:**

- 2 teaspoons extra-virgin olive oil
- 2 leeks, white parts only, sliced
- 1 apple, diced
- 2 cups cooked couscous
- 2 tablespoons curry powder
- ½ cup chopped pecans

**<u>Directions</u>:**

1. Warm-up the olive oil in a skillet over medium heat until shimmering. Add the leeks and sauté for 5 minutes or until soft.
2. Add the diced apple and cook for 3 more minutes until tender. Add the couscous and curry powder. Stir to combine.
3. Transfer them to a large serving bowl, then mix in the pecans and serve.

Nutrition: Calories: 254; Fat: 11.9 g; Protein: 5.4 g; Carbs: 34.3 g; Fiber: 5.9 g; Sodium: 15 mg

# Lemony Farro and Avocado Bowl

Prep & Cooking Time: 30 minutes

Servings: 4

## Ingredients:

- 1 tbsp & 2 tbsp extra-virgin olive oil, divided
- ½ medium onion, chopped
- 1 carrot, shredded
- 2 garlic cloves, minced
- 1 (6-ounce / 170-g) cup pearled farro
- 2 cups low-sodium vegetable soup
- 2 avocados, peeled, pitted, and sliced
- Zest and juice of 1 small lemon
- ¼ teaspoon of sea salt

## Directions:

1. Heat 1 tablespoon of olive oil in a saucepan over medium-high heat until shimmering.

2. Put the onion, then sauté for 5 minutes or until translucent. Add the carrot and garlic and sauté for 1 minute or until fragrant.

3. Add the farro and pour in the vegetable soup. Bring to a boil over high heat. Reduce the heat to low. Put the lid on and simmer for 20 minutes or until the farro is al dente.

4. Transfer it to a large bowl, then fold in the avocado slices. Sprinkle with lemon zest and salt, then drizzle with lemon juice and 2 teaspoons of olive oil. Stir to mix well and serve immediately.

Nutrition: Calories: 210; Fat: 11.1 g; Protein: 4.2 g; Carbs: 27.9 g; Fiber: 7.0 g; Sodium: 152 mg

## Rice and Blueberry Stuffed Sweet Potatoes

Prep & Cooking Time: 35 minutes

Servings: 4

**<u>Ingredients</u>:**

- 2 cups cooked wild rice
- ½ cup dried blueberries
- ½ cup chopped hazelnuts
- ½ cup shredded Swiss chard
- 1 teaspoon chopped fresh thyme
- 1 scallion, white and green parts, peeled and thinly sliced
- Sea salt and freshly ground black pepper, to taste
- 4 sweet potatoes, baked in the skin until tender

**Directions**:

1. Preheat the oven to 400°F (205°C).

2. Combine all the ingredients, except for the sweet potatoes, in a large bowl. Stir to mix well.

3. Cut the top third of the sweet potato off length wire, then scoop most of the sweet potato flesh out.

4. Fill the potato with the wild rice mixture, then set the sweet potato on a greased baking sheet.

5. Bake in the preheated oven for 20 minutes or until the sweet potato skin is lightly charred. Serve immediately.

Nutrition: Calories: 393; Fat: 7.1 g; Protein: 10.2 g; Carbs: 76.9 g; Fiber: 10.0 g; Sodium: 93 mg

## Mediterranean Lentils and Rice

Prep & Cooking Time: 30 minutes

Servings: 4

**Ingredients**:

- 2¼ cups low-sodium or no-salt-added vegetable broth
- ½ cup uncooked brown or green lentils
- ½ cup uncooked instant brown rice
- ½ cup diced carrots (about one carrot)
- ½ cup diced celery (about one stalk)
- 1 (2.25-ounce) can of sliced olives, drained (about ½ cup)

- ¼ cup diced red onion (about 1/8 onion)
- ¼ cup chopped fresh curly-leaf parsley
- 1½ tablespoons extra-virgin olive oil
- 1 tablespoon freshly squeezed lemon juice
- 1 garlic clove, minced (about ½ teaspoon)
- ¼ teaspoon kosher or sea salt
- ¼ teaspoon freshly ground black pepper

### Directions:

1. In a pan over high heat, bring the broth and lentils to a boil, cover, and lower the medium-low heat. Cook for 8 minutes.

2. Increase the setting to medium, and stir in the rice. Cover the pot and cook the mixture for 15 minutes, or until the liquid is absorbed. Take away the pot from the heat and let it sit, covered, for 1 minute, then stir.

3. Mix the carrots, celery, olives, onion, and parsley in a large serving bowl.

4. In a bowl, stick together the oil, lemon juice, garlic, salt, and pepper. Set aside.

5. While the lentils and rice are cooked, add them to the serving bowl. Transfer the dressing on top, and mix everything. Serve warm or cold, or store in a sealed container in the refrigerator for up to 7 days.

Nutrition: Calories: 230; Total Fat: 8 g; Total Carbohydrates: 34 g; Fiber: 6 g; Protein: 8 g

# Brown Rice Pilaf with Golden Raisins

Prep & Cooking Time: 30 minutes

Servings: 4

## Ingredients:

- 1 tablespoon of extra-virgin olive oil
- 1 cup of chopped onion (about ½ medium onion)
- ½ cup shredded carrot (about one medium carrot)
- 1 teaspoon of ground cumin
- ½ teaspoon ground cinnamon
- 2 cups instant brown rice
- 1¾ cups 100% orange juice
- ¼ cup of water
- 1 cup of golden raisins
- ½ cup shelled pistachios
- Chopped fresh chives (optional)

## Directions:

1. In a pan over medium-high heat, warm the oil. Add the onion, then cook for 5 minutes, stirring frequently. Add the carrot, cumin, and cinnamon, and cook for 1 minute, stirring frequently. Stir in the rice, orange juice, and water. Let it boil, cover, then lower the heat to medium-low. Simmer for 7 minutes, or until the rice is cooked through and the liquid is absorbed.

2. Stir in the raisins, pistachios, and chives (if using) and serve.

Nutrition: Calories: 320; Total Fat: 7 g; Total Carbohydrates: 61 g; Fiber: 5 g; Protein: 6 g

# Lebanese Rice and Broken Noodles with Cabbage

Prep & Cooking Time: 30 minutes

Servings: 4

## Ingredients:

- 1 tablespoon of extra-virgin olive oil
- 1 cup (about 3 ounces) uncooked vermicelli or thin spaghetti, broken into 1- to 1½-inch pieces
- 3 cups shredded cabbage (about half a 14-ounce package of coleslaw mix or half a small head of cabbage)
- 3 cups low-sodium or no-salt-added vegetable broth
- ½ cup of water
- 1 cup of instant brown rice
- 2 garlic cloves
- ¼ teaspoon kosher or sea salt
- 1/8 to ¼ teaspoon crushed red pepper
- ½ cup loosely packed, coarsely chopped cilantro
- Fresh lemon slices, for serving (optional)

## Directions:

1. In a pan over medium heat, pour the oil.

2. Put the pasta and cook for 3 minutes to toast, stirring often. Add the cabbage and cook for 4 minutes, stirring frequently. Add the broth, water, rice, garlic, salt, and crushed red pepper, and bring to a boil over high heat. Stir, close the lid and reduce the heat to medium-low. Simmer for 10 minutes.

3. Remove the pan from the heat, but do not lift the lid. Let sit for 5 minutes. Fish out the garlic cloves, mash them with a fork, then stir the garlic back into the rice. Stir in the cilantro. Serve with lemon slices (if using).

Nutrition: Calories: 259; Total Fat: 4 g; Total Carbohydrates: 49 g; Fiber: 3 g; Protein: 7 g

## Barley Risotto with Parmesan

Prep & Cooking Time: 30 minutes

Servings: 4

## Ingredients:

- 4 cups low-sodium or no-salt-added vegetable broth
- 1 tablespoon of extra-virgin olive oil
- 1 cup of chopped yellow onion (about ½ medium onion)
- 2 cups uncooked pearl barley
- ½ cup dry white wine
- 1 cup freshly grated Parmesan cheese (about 4 ounces), divided
- ¼ teaspoon kosher or sea salt
- ¼ teaspoon freshly ground black pepper
- Fresh chopped chives and lemon wedges, for serving (optional)

## Directions:

1. Pour the broth into a medium saucepan and bring to a simmer.

2. In a pot over medium heat, pour the oil.

3. Add the onion and cook for 8 minutes, stirring occasionally. Add the barley, then cook it for 2 minutes, stirring until the barley is toasted. Pour in the wine and cook for about 1 minute or until most of the liquid evaporates. Add one cup of hot broth into the pot and cook, stirring for about 2 minutes, or wait until most of the liquid is absorbed. Add the remaining broth 1 cup at a time, cooking until each cup is absorbed (about 2 minutes each time) before adding the next. The last addition of broth will take a bit longer to absorb, about 4 minutes.

4. Take away the pot from the heat, stir in ½ cup of cheese and salt and pepper. Serve with the lasting cheese on the side, along with the chives and lemon wedges (if using).

Nutrition: Calories: 346; Total Fat: 7 g; Total Carbohydrates: 56 g; Fiber: 11 g; Protein: 14 g

## Garlic-Asparagus Israeli Couscous

Prep & Cooking Time: 30 minutes

Servings: 4

**Ingredients**:

- 1 cup garlic-and-herb goat cheese (about 4 ounces)
- 1½ pounds asparagus spears end trimmed and stalks chopped into 1-inch pieces (about 2¾ to 3 cups chopped)
- 1 tablespoon of extra-virgin olive oil
- 1 garlic clove, minced (about ½ teaspoon)
- ¼ teaspoon freshly ground black pepper

- 1¾ cups water
- 1 (8-ounce) box uncooked whole-wheat or regular Israeli couscous (almost 11/3 cups)
- ¼ teaspoon kosher or sea salt

## Directions:

1. Preheat the oven to 425°F. Put the goat cheese on the counter to bring to room temperature.

2. In a large bowl, mix the asparagus, oil, garlic, and pepper. Put the asparagus on a baking sheet, then roast for 10 minutes, stirring a few times. Take away the pan from the oven, and spoon the asparagus into a large serving bowl.

3. While the asparagus is roasting, in a medium saucepan, bring the water to a boil. Add the couscous and salt. Lessen the heat to medium-low, cover, and cook for 12 minutes, or until the water is absorbed.

4. Pour the hot couscous into the bowl with the asparagus. Add the goat cheese, mix thoroughly until completely melted, and serve.

Nutrition: Calories: 263; Total Fat: 9 g; Total Carbohydrates: 36 g; Fiber: 3 g; Protein: 11 g

# Tangy Tilapia Fish Fillets with Crusty Coating

Prep & Cooking Time: 15 minutes

Servings: 4

## Ingredients:

- ¼-cup ground flaxseed
- 1-cup almonds, finely chopped (divided)
- 4-6 oz. tilapia fillets
- ½-tsp salt
- 2-tbsp olive oil

## Directions:

1. Combine the flaxseed with half of the almonds in a shallow mixing bowl to serve as a crusty coating instead of a flour mixture.

2. Sprinkle the tilapia fillets evenly with salt. Dredge the fillet in the flaxseed-almond mixture. Set aside.

3. Heat the olive oil in a heavy, thick-bottomed skillet placed over medium heat. Add the coated fillets, and cook for 4 minutes on each side until golden brown, flipping once. Remove the fillets, and transfer them to a serving plate.

4. In the same skillet, add the remaining almonds. Toast for a minute until turning golden brown, stirring frequently. Sprinkle the toasted almonds over the fish fillets.

Nutrition: Calories: 258; Total Fats: 21.3 g; Dietary Fiber: 4.9 g; Carbohydrates: 7.1 g; Protein: 11.6 g

# Feta-Fused Mussels Marmite

Prep & Cooking Time: 30 minutes

Servings: 6

## Ingredients:

- 2-tbsp olive oil
- 1-pc medium onion, chopped
- 1-cup white wine
- ½-tsp salt
- 2-lbs mussels (without the shell)
- 1-dash of cayenne pepper
- 2-cloves of garlic, chopped
- 1-tbsp tomato paste
- 2-oz of feta cheese grated
- Bunch of parsley, chopped

## Directions:

1. Preheat your oven to 400 °F.

2. Heat the oil in a large pot placed over medium-high heat and sauté the onion for 3 minutes until tender. Pour the white wine, and add the tomato, salt, and mussels. Bring to a boil until all the mussels break open and the wine evaporates.

3. Add the cayenne and garlic. Simmer for 5 minutes.

4. Take out the top shell of the mussels. Sprinkle the opened mussels with feta cheese and parsley.

5. Place the pot in the preheated oven—grill for 8 minutes until the cheese begins to melt and appear with a golden color.

Nutrition: Calories: 227; Total Fats: 10.1 g; Dietary Fiber: 0.6 g; Carbohydrates: 9.8 g; Protein: 19.8 g

## Sauced Shellfish in White Wine

Prep & Cooking Time: 20 minutes

Servings: 6

### Ingredients:

- 2-lbs fresh cuttlefish
- ½-cup olive oil
- 1-pc large onion, finely chopped
- 1-cup of Robola white wine
- ¼-cup lukewarm water
- 1-pc bay leaf
- ½-bunch parsley, chopped
- 4-pcs tomatoes, grated
- Salt and pepper

**Directions**:

1. Take out the hard centerpiece of cartilage (cuttlebone), the bag of ink, and the intestines from the cuttlefish. Wash the cleaned cuttlefish with running water. Slice it into small pieces, and drain excess water.

2. Heat the oil in a saucepan placed over medium-high heat and sauté the onion for 3 minutes until tender.

3. Add the sliced cuttlefish and pour in the white wine. Cook for 5 minutes until it simmers.

4. Pour in the water, then add the tomatoes, bay leaf, parsley, tomatoes, salt, and pepper. Simmer the mixture over low heat until the cuttlefish slices are tender and left with their thick sauce. Serve them warm with rice.

Nutrition: Calories: 308; Total Fats: 18.1 g; Dietary Fiber: 1.5 g; Carbohydrates: 8 g; Protein: 25.6 g

## Baked Butterflied Trout Treat with Florence Fennel

Prep & Cooking Time: 40 minutes

Servings: 6

**Ingredients**:

For the Florence Fennel Salad:

- 2-bulbs fennel, thinly sliced
- 2-tbsp capers
- 1-lemon, juiced
- ¼-cup parsley leaves

- 2-tbsp extra-virgin olive oil
- 1-tsp kosher salt
- Freshly ground pepper

For the Fish:

- 6-pcs whole small trout, cleaned and butterflied
- 12-sprigs fresh oregano (divided)
- 1-pc small bunch parsley
- 1-bulb small red onion, peeled and sliced
- 1-pc large lemon, thinly sliced
- Salt and pepper
- ¼-cup extra-virgin olive oil

### **Directions**:

For the Salad:

1. Combine all the fennel salad ingredients in a small mixing bowl. Mix well until thoroughly combined. Set aside.

For the Fish:

1. Preheat your oven to 400 °F.

2. Lay the butterflied trout on a greased baking sheet. Stuff each trout with 2-whole sprigs of oregano and parsley and slices of red onion and lemon. Sprinkle with salt and pepper, and shower with olive oil.

3. Place the baking sheet in the preheated oven. Bake for 18 minutes until the trout is firm and flaky. Serve with the fennel salad.

Nutrition: Calories: 580; Total Fats: 34 g; Dietary Fiber: 5 g; Carbohydrates: 10 g; Protein: 61 g

# Chapter 4:
# Dessert

## Fresh Figs with Walnuts and Ricotta

Prep & Cooking Time: 10 minutes

Servings: 4

## Ingredients:

- 8 dried figs, halved
- ¼ cup of ricotta cheese
- 16 walnuts, halved
- 1 tablespoon of honey

## Directions:

1. Take a skillet and place it over medium heat, add walnuts and toast for 2 minutes.

2. Top figs with cheese and walnuts.

3. Drizzle honey on top. Enjoy!

Nutrition: Calories: 142; Fat: 8 g; Carbohydrates:10 g; Protein: 4 g; Sodium: 5%

# Authentic Medjool Date Truffles

Prep & Cooking Time: 10 minutes

Servings: 4

**Ingredients**:

- 2 tablespoons of peanut oil
- ½ cup of popcorn kernels
- 1/3 cup of peanuts, chopped
- 1/3 cup of peanut almond butter
- ¼ cup of wildflower honey

**Directions**:

1. Take a pot and add popcorn kernels, peanut oil.

2. Place it over medium heat and shake the pot gently until all corn has popped.

3. Take a saucepan and add honey, gently simmer for 2-3 minutes.

4. Add peanut almond butter and stir.

5. Coat popcorn with the mixture and enjoy!

Nutrition: Calories: 430; Fat: 20 g; Carbohydrates: 56 g; Protein: 9 g; Sodium: 69%

# Tasty Mediterranean Peanut Almond Butter Popcorns

Prep & Cooking Time: 30 minutes

Servings: 4

**Ingredients**:

- 3 cups of Medjool dates, chopped
- 12 ounces of brewed coffee
- 1 cup of pecans, chopped
- ½ cup of coconut, shredded
- ½ cup of cocoa powder

**Directions**:

1. Soak dates in warm coffee for 5 minutes.

2. Remove dates from coffee and mash them, making a fine smooth mixture.

3. Stir in remaining ingredients (except cocoa powder) and form small balls out of the mixture.

4. Coat with cocoa powder, serve and enjoy!

Nutrition: Calories: 265; Fat: 12 g; Carbohydrates: 43 g; Protein: 3 g; Sodium: 9%

# Just a Minute Worth Muffin

Prep & Cooking Time: 10 minutes

Servings: 2

## Ingredients:

- Coconut oil for grease
- 2 teaspoons of coconut flour
- 1 pinch of baking soda
- 1 pinch of sunflower seeds
- 1 whole egg

## Directions:

1. Grease ramekin dish with coconut oil and keep it on the side.

2. Add ingredients to a bowl and combine until no lumps.

3. Pour batter into the ramekin. Microwave for 1 minute on HIGH.

4. Slice in half and serve.

5. Enjoy!

Nutrition: Calories: 155; Total Carbs: 5.4 g; Fiber: 2 g; Protein: 7.3 g; Sodium: 8%

# Lemon Granita

Prep & Cooking Time: 15 minutes

Servings: 10

## Ingredients:

- 4 fresh lemons, juice about 3/4 cup
- 1 ½ cups of natural sweetener (Stevia, Erythritol...etc.)
- 3 cups of water
- 2 lemon peeled, pulp

## Directions:

1. In a saucepan, heat all ingredients over medium heat.

2. Remove from heat and let cool at room temperature.

3. Pour the mixture into a baking dish, wrap with a plastic membrane and freeze for 6 - 8 hours.

4. Remove granite from the freezer, scratch with a big fork, and stir.

5. Serve in chilled glasses and enjoy!

6. Keep in the freezer.

Nutrition: Calories: 13; Carbohydrates: 3 g; Proteins: 1 g; Fat: 1 g; Fiber: 0.2 g; Sodium: 3%

**Pumpkin Pie**

Prep & Cooking Time: 60 minutes

Servings: 8

## Ingredients:

- 1 cup of ginger snaps
- ½ cup of egg white
- 16 ounces of canned pumpkin
- ½ cup of sugar
- 2 teaspoons of pumpkin pie spice
- 12 ounces of (can) skim milk, evaporated

## Directions:

1. Using a food processor, grind the cookies thoroughly.

2. Set the oven to 350°F and preheat.

3. Take a 10" glass pie pan and sprinkle little vegetable cooking oil.

4. Spread the cookie crumbs evenly in the pan.

5. In a medium mixing bowl, combine all the remaining.

6. Pour over the crust and bake.

7. Continue baking for about 45 minutes, until you can insert a knife and take it out clean.

8. Once it is baked well, allow it cool and refrigerate.

9. Slice it into eight wedges.

Nutrition: Calories: 184; Total Carbs: 39.4 g; Total Fat: 0.5 g; Cholesterol: 2 mg; Sodium: 84 mg

Dietary Fiber: 3.4 g; Sugars: 33.3 g; Calcium: 144 mg; Potassium: 424 mg; Iron: 2 mg

## Yogurt with Honey and Strawberries

Prep & Cooking Time: 15 minutes

Servings: 2

<u>**Ingredients**</u>:

- 2 teaspoons of honey
- 2 tablespoons of toasted almonds, sliced
- 8 ounces of fresh strawberries
- 1½ cups of yogurt, low-fat, plain

<u>**Directions**</u>:

1. Prepare the strawberries by cleaning and slicing them into quarters. Keep it ready aside.

2. Divide the yogurt into two serving cups. Put the strawberries equally into the cups.

3. Top it with honey. Dress it with almonds. Serve fresh.

Nutrition: Calories: 223; Total Carbs: 28.7 g; Total Fat: 5.6 g; Cholesterol: 11 mg; Sodium: 130 mg; Dietary Fiber: 3 g; Total Sugars: 24.5 g; Protein: 12.5 g; Calcium: 371 mg; Iron: 1 mg; Potassium: 651 mg

## Milk Chocolate Pudding

Prep & Cooking Time: 30 minutes

Servings: 2

### Ingredients:

- 1½ tablespoons corn starch
- 1 tablespoon of sugar
- 1 tablespoon of cocoa powder
- 1 cup of milk, fatless
- 5½ tablespoons chocolate chips
- ¼ teaspoon vanilla
- ¼ teaspoon salt

### Directions:

1. Combine corn starch, sugar, cocoa powder, and salt thoroughly in a medium bowl. Add milk and mix thoroughly.

2. Place a medium saucepan over medium heat and pour the mix into the pan.

3. Stir under medium heat continuously, until it becomes into a thick consistency and starts to bubble. When it starts to bubble, remove it from the heat.

4. Add vanilla and chocolate chips and stir to become a smooth paste. Transfer the mix into two serving cups and allow to set.

5. Place a plastic wrap over the surface of the pudding to stop it from forming.

6. Serve fresh or refrigerate and serve.

Nutrition: Calories: 250; Total Carbs: 36.1 g; Total Fat: 9.1 g; Cholesterol: 9 mg; Sodium: 235 mg; Dietary Fiber: 1.8 g; Total Sugars: 27.2 g; Protein: 6.9 g; Calcium: 209 mg; Iron: 1 mg; Potassium: 380 mg

## Strawberry-Pear Trifle

Prep & Cooking Time: 10 minutes

Servings: 5

### Ingredients:

- 1 cup of strawberries, finely chopped
- 1 pear, cored, thinly sliced
- 1 tablespoon of lemon juice
- 1 tablespoon of orange juice
- ¼ teaspoon of almond extract
- 1½ cups of yogurt, vanilla-flavored
- 1 tablespoon of honey
- 3 inches food cake, 1-inch cube cuts
- Mint springs and pear slices – for garnishing

**Directions**:

1. In a large bowl put pears, strawberries.

2. Pour lemon juice and almond extract and toss well.

3. Add honey, orange juice, and stir well.

4. Take a 2-quart glass bowl and layer as follows. A quarter of cake drizzled with orange juice mixture, quarter cup yogurt, quarter cup pear slices, and quarter cup strawberries. Repeat the layering in the same format.

5. Layer the balance of cake sprinkled with orange juice mixture. Spread the remaining yogurt on top. Cover it with plastic wrap and refrigerate for about 1 to 4 hours.

6. Garnish with mint and pear slice before serving.

Nutrition: Calories: 94; Total Carbs: 15.6 g; Total Fat: 1.1 g; Cholesterol: 4 mg; Sodium: 53 mg;

Dietary Fiber: 1.5 g; Total Sugars: 13.2 g; Protein: 4.5 g; Calcium: 142mg; Iron: 0 mg; Potassium: 261 mg

# Chocolate Pudding without Lactose

Prep & Cooking Time: 35 minutes

Servings: 8

## Ingredients:

- ¼ cup of corn starch
- 4 cups of milk, low-fat, lactose-free
- ¼ cup of cocoa powder, unsweetened
- 2 ounces of chocolate, finely chopped
- ¼ cups + 2 tablespoons of sugar
- 1 teaspoon of vanilla extract
- ¼ teaspoon of kosher salt

## Directions:

1. Blend corn starch and ½ cup of milk in a medium bowl. Take another bowl and mix thoroughly cocoa and salt.

2. Add the remaining milk, sugar, and chocolate and combine thoroughly.

3. Pour the second batch mix in a 9" saucepan and heat over medium temperature and stir continuously until the chocolate melt well.

4. Add the first blend of corn starch mixture into the saucepan and stir. Continue cooking at low heat until the mixture becomes thick.

5. Continue cooking until it starts to bubble.

6. At this junction, remove the pan from the heat and add the vanilla extract. Combine it and allow it to cool.

7. When it is cold, transfer into custard cups. Cover it with plastic wrap and refrigerate before serving. Allow it to set and serve.

Nutrition: Calories: 129; Total Carbs: 20.7 g   Total Fat: 4 g; Sodium: 135 mg; Dietary Fiber: 1.1 g; Total Sugars: 15 g; Protein: 4 g; Calcium: 142 mg, Iron: 1 mg; Potassium: 95 mg

## Low Carb Blackberry Ice Cream

Prep & Cooking Time: 10 minutes

Servings: 8

### Ingredients:

- 3/4 lbs. of frozen blackberries, unsweetened
- 1 1/4 cup of canned coconut milk
- 1/4 cup of granulated Stevia sweetener or to taste
- 2 tbsp. of almond flour
- 1 pinch of ground vanilla
- 1 tbsp. of MCT oil

### Directions:

1. Put all the ingredients in a blender. Make sure blackberries are still frozen.

2. Blend until the mixture is creamy.

3. Pour the blackberry mixture into a container and freeze overnight.

4. Serve in chilled glasses or bowls.

Nutrition: Calories: 83; Carbohydrates: 5 g; Proteins: 1 g; Fat: 8 g; Fiber: 2.5 g; Sodium: 10%

## Peach and Blueberry Tart

Prep & Cooking Time: 40 minutes

Servings: 6-8

### Ingredients:

- 1 sheet frozen puff pastry
- 1 cup of fresh blueberries
- 4 peaches, pitted and sliced
- 3 tablespoons of sugar
- 2 tablespoons of cornstarch
- 1 tablespoon of freshly squeezed lemon juice
- Cooking spray
- 1 tablespoon of nonfat or low-fat milk
- Confectioners' sugar, for dusting

### Directions:

1. Thaw puff pastry at room temperature for at least 30 minutes.

2. Preheat the oven to 400°F.

3. In a large bowl, toss the blueberries, peaches, sugar, cornstarch, and lemon juice.

4. Spray a round pie pan with cooking spray. Unfold pastry and place on the prepared pie pan.

5. Arrange the peach slices, so they are slightly overlapping. Spread the blueberries on top of the peaches.

6. Drape pastry over the outside of the fruit and press pleats firmly together. Brush with milk. Bake in the bottom third of the oven until crust is golden, about 30 minutes. Cool on a rack.

7. Sprinkle pastry with confectioners' sugar. Serve.

Nutrition: Total Calories: 119; Total Fat: 3 g Sodium: 21 mg Potassium: 155 mg Total Carbohydrate: 23 g; Cholesterol: 0 mg; Fiber: 2 g; Sugars: 15 g; Saturated Fat: 1 g; Protein: 1 g

## Sriracha Parsnip Fries

Prep & Cooking Time: 35 minutes

Servings: 4

**Ingredients**:

- 1-pound parsnips, peeled, cut into 3 × ½-inch strips
- 1 tablespoon of olive oil
- 1 teaspoon of dried rosemary
- Sriracha to taste
- Salt and pepper to taste

1. Preheat oven to 450°F.

2. Mix parsnips, rosemary, and oil in a medium-sized bowl. Season with salt, pepper, and Sriracha to taste and toss to coat.

3. Lay parsnips on a baking sheet making sure the strips don't overlap. (If they are touching, they will become mushy instead of crispy.)

4. Bake for 10 minutes. Turn and roast until parsnips are browned in spots, 10 to 15 minutes longer. If you want them to be extra crispy, turn the broiler on for the last 2 to 3 minutes.

5. Remove from oven and enjoy.

Nutrition: Total Calories: 112; Total Fat: 4 g; Saturated Fat: 1 g; Cholesterol: 0 mg; Sodium: 12 mg

Potassium: 419 mg; Carbohydrate: 20 g; Fiber: 4 g; Sugars: 5 g; Protein: 2 g

## Yogurt Parfait with Lime and Grapefruit

Prep & Cooking Time: 25 minutes

Servings: 6

**Ingredients**:

- 3 tablespoons of honey
- 2 tablespoons of lime juice
- 2 teaspoons of grated lime zest
- Fresh mint leaves (torn)
- 4 cups of plain yogurt (reduced-fat)
- 4 large red grapefruit

## Directions:

1. Cut a small part of each grapefruit's top and bottom. Make them stand on a cutting board. Cut off peel and gently slice through the membrane of the fruit's segment to get the fruit.

2. Put juice, lime zest, and yogurt in a bowl. Arrange half of the grapefruit in 6 parfait glasses. Top each glass with half of the yogurt mixture. Repeat until you have no more fruit and yogurt mixture left. Top each glass with honey and mint.

Nutrition: Calories: 207; Protein: 7.12 g; Fat: 5.53 g; Carbohydrates: 34.71 g; Sodium: 115 mg

## Fruit and Nut Bites

Prep & Cooking Time: 1 hour

Servings: 4 dozen

## Ingredients:

- 1 cup of pistachios (toasted and finely chopped)
- 1 cup of dried cherries (finely chopped)
- 2 cups of dried apricots (finely chopped)
- 1/4 cup of honey
- 1/4 teaspoon of almond extract
- 3 3/4 cups sliced almonds (divided)

**Directions**:

1. Put 1 1/4 cups of almonds in a food processor. Pulse until chopped. Transfer to a bowl and set aside.

2. Process 2 1/2 cups almonds in a food processor until chopped. Gradually add extract and honey as you process. Transfer to a bowl. Add cherries and apricots. Divide into 6 and shape them into thick rolls. Wrap in plastic and leave it in the fridge for an hour.

3. Remove plastic and cut each roll to 1 1/2-inch piece. Roll half of them in pistachios. Roll the other half in almonds. Wrap each piece in waxed paper and store it in an airtight container.

Nutrition: Calories: 86; Protein: 9.22 g; Fat: 14.95 g; Carbohydrates: 72.36 g; Sodium: 15 mg

# Measurement Conversions

## Volume Equivalents (Liquid)

| STANDARD | US STANDARD (OUNCES) | METRIC (APPROXIMATE) |
|---|---|---|
| 2 tablespoons | 1 fl. oz. | 30 mL |
| ¼ cup | 2 fl. oz. | 60 mL |
| ½ cup | 4 fl. oz. | 120 mL |
| 1 cup | 8 fl. oz. | 240 mL |
| 1½ cups | 12 fl. oz. | 355 mL |
| 2 cups or 1 pint | 16 fl. oz. | 475 mL |
| 4 cups or 1 quart | 32 fl. oz. | 1 L |
| 1 gallon | 128 fl. oz. | 4 L |

# Volume Equivalents (Dry)

| STANDARD | METRIC (APPROXIMATE) |
|---|---|
| ⅛ teaspoon | 0.5 mL |
| ¼ teaspoon | 1 mL |
| ½ teaspoon | 2 mL |
| ¾ teaspoon | 4 mL |
| 1 teaspoon | 5 mL |
| 1 tablespoon | 15 mL |
| ¼ cup | 59 mL |
| ⅓ cup | 79 mL |
| ½ cup | 118 mL |
| ⅔ cup | 156 mL |
| ¾ cup | 177 mL |
| 1 cup | 235 mL |
| 2 cups or 1 pint | 475 mL |
| 3 cups | 700 mL |
| 4 cups or 1 quart | 1 L |

## Oven Temperatures

| FAHRENHEIT (F) | CELSIUS (C) (APPROXIMATE) |
|---|---|
| 250°F | 120°C |
| 300°F | 150°C |
| 325°F | 165°C |
| 350°F | 180°C |
| 375°F | 190°C |
| 400°F | 200°C |
| 425°F | 220°C |
| 450°F | 230°C |

## Weight Equivalents

| STANDARD | METRIC (APPROXIMATE) |
|---|---|
| ½ ounce | 15 g |
| 1 ounce | 30 g |
| 2 ounces | 60 g |
| 4 ounces | 115 g |
| 8 ounces | 225 g |
| 12 ounces | 340 g |
| 16 ounces or 1 pound | 455 g |

Printed in Great Britain
by Amazon